CONTENTS

WHAT IS AN EVO?

The Gogo's have evolved new characters, new skills and new things for you to look out for.

Get to know your new Gogo's and learn how to spot an official Evolution Gogo's Crazy Bone.

MOSHI 01

Avoids confrontation. Always brings goodness and peace.

SPECIAL ABILITY:
Peacemaker

FAVOURITE GAME: K.O.

EVOLUTION: 15

TRANSPARENT EVOLUTION

You can recognize the Gogo's with TRANSPARENT EVOLUTION by this symbol.

MOSHI 01

Avoids confrontation. Always brings goodness and peace.

SPECIAL ABILITY:
Peacemaker

FAVOURITE GAME: K.O.

NAME AND NUMBER

Every Gogo has a name and number. You'll find all their names in this handbook. If you look closely at the back of your Gogo, you'll find its number printed just above the MAGIC BOX INT. stamp.

GOGO PERSONALITIES

Each Gogo is very special and has its own personality and special abilities. If you want to know more about them, you can read their profiles right here in this handbook. You'll also find information on each of the Gogo's favourite games.

HOW TO PLAY?

You'll never be bored with a Gogo; there are so many games to play!
Different Gogo's are better for playing different games depending on
their size, shape and weight. Check out the profiles and use the handy
guide to find out which games will best suit your Gogo's.

EVOLUTION BAR

Gogo's have EVOLVED! Use the EVOLUTION BAR
to see how much each character has evolved.

LEVEL 15 = MAXIMUM EVOLUTION

LEVEL 1 = MINIMUM EVOLUTION

COLOURS

Each Gogo is available in five different colours.
All the colours of every Gogo can be found at the
back of this handbook in the checklist section.

THE BACK

Look on the back of your Gogo's and you'll find they are all designed the
same so that you can hold them or throw them with just one finger.
Of course, practice is the key to becoming a Gogo champion.

DON'T ACCEPT IMITATIONS

Pick up a Gogo and turn it over to check that it has
the MAGIC BOX INT. stamp. The MAGIC BOX INT. stamp guarantees
that your Gogo is an original, has a fantastic bounce and is a bright, shiny colour.

The Gogo's have been allowed to run riot around the factory. The more mischievous members of the Gogo's have been messing with the machines in the factory and causing chaos.

Help the Gogo makers by finding out how many of each Gogo has been made.

 = | 2

 = 8

 = 8

 = 8

 = 8

FIND ALL THE ANSWERS ON PAGE 88

HELED'S QUIZ!

1 Which of these Gogo's does not have a transparent evolution?

A. Yonozi ✓

B. Sut

C. Sip

2 The Gogo's go crazy looking for him underwater, who is he?

Snok

3

Which Gogo wears this logo?

4 If you needed a Gogo for instant snacking, who would you choose?

A. Kingo

B. Imooki

C. Egor

5 What is B-Kori's favourite game to play?

FIND ALL THE ANSWERS ON PAGE 88

PROFILES

MOSHI 01

Avoids confrontation. Always brings goodness and peace.

SPECIAL ABILITY:
Peacemaker

FAVOURITE GAME: K.O.

EVOLUTION: **15**

02 NASOKI

Tries to make everyone laugh. Sometimes his looks scare the others a little bit.

SPECIAL ABILITY:
Joker

FAVOURITE GAME: Bowling

EVOLUTION: **11**

PROFILES

03 SATORI ♂

Always watchful in case action is needed.

SPECIAL ABILITY:
Watchful Eye

FAVOURITE GAME: Basket

EVOLUTION: 12

OKY 04 ♂

Maybe some indigestion gave him a mushroom face.

SPECIAL ABILITY:
Fungus Fury

FAVOURITE GAME: Bowling

EVOLUTION: 13

05 RACETOR ♂

He loves sports and can calculate how to win any race.

SPECIAL ABILITY:
Numeric Memory

FAVOURITE GAME: Scoring

55

EVOLUTION: 09

HELED 06 ♂

He robotized his brain to think super fast.

SPECIAL ABILITY:
Mental Dexterity

FAVOURITE GAME: K.O.

EVOLUTION: 08

PROFILES

07 SKER ♂

He's naive and everything seems weird to him.

SPECIAL ABILITY:
Curiosity

FAVOURITE GAME: In Flight

EVOLUTION: 10

08 ANGOR ♂

Night mysteries are no secret to Angor.

SPECIAL ABILITY:
Insomnia

FAVOURITE GAME: In Flight

EVOLUTION: 06

PROFILES

TAI-UMU 09

With the points of his mouth-star he chews the hardest things.

SPECIAL ABILITY:
Star Scream

FAVOURITE GAME: Bowling

EVOLUTION: **13**

KOKU-CHAN 10

He must go to the barber every day because his hair grows while he plays.

SPECIAL ABILITY:
Manic Hair

FAVOURITE GAME: In Flight

EVOLUTION: **13**

PROFILES

CHIRU 11

The moon reflects in his eyes when he's sleepy.

SPECIAL ABILITY:
Counting Sheep

FAVOURITE GAME: Basket

EVOLUTION: 08

NUCHAN 12

Serious and thoughtful. He acts like the chief Gogo.

SPECIAL ABILITY:
Action Planning

FAVOURITE GAME: On Line

EVOLUTION: 11

11

PROFILES

OM-POH 13

Uses spells to play better.
Sometimes it works.

SPECIAL ABILITY:
Multiple Faces

FAVOURITE GAME: Battle

EVOLUTION: 10

14 NEBUB

Concentrates the water supply
to put out any fire.

SPECIAL ABILITY:
Firefighting

FAVOURITE GAME: On Line

EVOLUTION: 09

PROFILES

HAZER 15

His game style is funny and he goes crazy watching others play.

SPECIAL ABILITY:
Unintentional Humour

FAVOURITE GAME: Battle

EVOLUTION: 11

SUNON 16

Ticklish all over his body. Nobody can even stand close to him.

SPECIAL ABILITY:
Ticklish

FAVOURITE GAME: Battle

EVOLUTION: 12

GAME RULES

BASEBALL

① Draw a baseball diamond on the ground. Decide who will be 'batter' and place that player's Gogo on the batting plate.

② That player then rolls four Gogo's and works out how far to move their Gogo using the score card below.

③ The player moves the Gogo's around the diamond the required number of spaces. Each time a Gogo makes a complete circuit of the diamond the player scores a point.

④ When the batter is out three times it is the other player's turn. The game can go on for any number of rounds, but the traditional number for a baseball game is nine. The winner is the player with the most points at the end of the game.

SCORE CARD

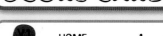

X1	HOME RUN	= 1 POINT
X4	HOME RUN	= 1 POINT
X3	TRIPLE	= MOVE 3 BASES
X2	DOUBLE	= MOVE 2 BASES
X1	SINGLE	= MOVE 1 BASE
X0	ZERO	= BATTER IS OUT!

GAME RULES

BATTLE

1 Two players arrange six or more of their Gogo's in parallel rows a short distance apart.

2 Players must decide before the start of the match how many throws there will be.

3 Players then throw their Gogo at their opponent's row and attempt to knock Gogo's out of the line.

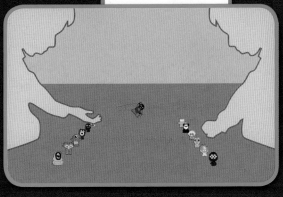

4 The player who knocks down the most of their opponent's Gogo's wins.

TIPS

If using basic rules, the Gogo's do not need to fall over completely, but simply be knocked out of the line.

If you want to play advanced rules, then the Gogo's must actually be knocked over as well as being pushed out of the line.

15

GOGO GAMES!

THE GOGO

Some of the Gogo's have been getting themselves into trouble and need your help to prove they are innocent. The authorities have a snapshot of their suspect but need your help in narrowing down which one of the Evolution Gogo's they are after.

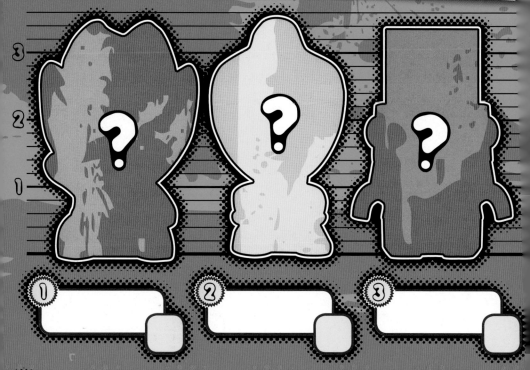

SUSPECTS!

Using the line-up of suspects, see if you can name all the Gogo's that have been called in for questioning and put a tick in the box next to who you think the main troublemaker is.

4

5

6

FIND ALL THE ANSWERS ON PAGE 89

NASOKI'S JOKES!

Why are pirates so mean?

I don't know, they just **ARRRRe!**

What did the lion say when he saw the boy go past on his skateboard?

Eat up your spinach, it'll put colour in your cheeks.

Meals on Wheels!

But I don't want green cheeks!

CRAZY TOUCH

1 Take a box – a shoebox will do – and place at least 10 Gogo's inside.

2 Each player takes turns to reach into the box with their eyes covered and pick up a Gogo.

3 With their eyes still covered, the player must guess which Gogo they have in their hand by feeling it. A correct guess scores a point. The first player to get 10 points wins.

TIP

If you want to make the game even more difficult, the first player to get 10 points in a row wins.

4 Give the box a shake between turns to mix the Gogo's up.

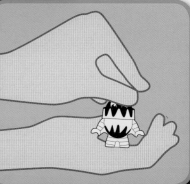

HELED'S QUIZ!

1 Can you name the two Gogo's who have got into a bit of a mix-up here?

A.

B.

2 Which Gogo does not like Bowling?

A. Sip

B. Kivu

C. Triku

3 If you add Temsei's Gogo number to Mizu's, what do you get?

A. 48

B. 72

C. 96

4 If you saw this, which Gogo would you be looking at?

5 What is Koku-Chan's special ability?

FIND ALL THE ANSWERS ON PAGE 89

LOST GOGO'S®

GOGO GAMES!

The Gogo's have been invited to an amazing party, but some of them have lost their invites with the maps to get to the party.

Can you help the Gogo's find their missing invites?

START

FINISH

FIND ALL THE ANSWERS ON PAGE 90

PROFILES

17 HIROKI

Never afraid of new games.
Always on the front line.

SPECIAL ABILITY:
Bravery

FAVOURITE GAME: On Line

EVOLUTION: 14

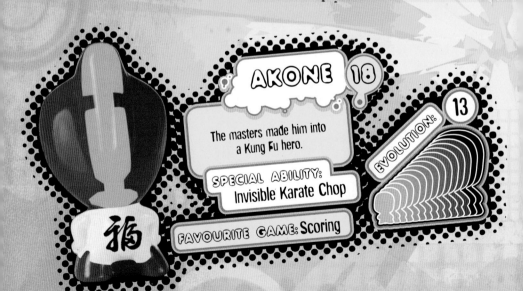

AKONE 18

The masters made him into
a Kung Fu hero.

SPECIAL ABILITY:
Invisible Karate Chop

FAVOURITE GAME: Scoring

EVOLUTION: 13

PROFILES

19 SULLY

The energy of the stars is always with him. . . or so he says.

SPECIAL ABILITY: Force Concentrator

FAVOURITE GAME: Basket

EVOLUTION: 10

NARION 20

He shows himself in darkness thanks to his glowing glasses.

SPECIAL ABILITY: Particle Searcher

FAVOURITE GAME: Battle

EVOLUTION: 08

PROFILES

SIMSEI 21 ♂

His mouth acts like a freezer and he's always shivering.

SPECIAL ABILITY: Walking Freezer

FAVOURITE GAME: Basket

EVOLUTION: 04

22 DOKI ♂

He has an incredibly sweet tooth. When he's not playing he's hunting for sweets.

SPECIAL ABILITY: Sweet Gobbler

FAVOURITE GAME: Basket

EVOLUTION: 12

PROFILES

23 HIRCHAN ♂

No hook and no eye-patch but this pirate is still sailing the high seas.

SPECIAL ABILITY:
Treasure Finder

FAVOURITE GAME: Scoring

EVOLUTION: 05

24 RUFISTAR ♂

He's the main attraction at any party. Creates fun for everyone.

SPECIAL ABILITY:
Hell Raiser

FAVOURITE GAME: Battle

EVOLUTION: 11

25 TEMSEI

He's a real handyman.
He can fix anything. . .
except his own shoelaces!

SPECIAL ABILITY:
Fixer Fantastic

FAVOURITE GAME: Scoring

EVOLUTION: 11

PILHY 26

He's got a positive pole, a negative
pole and he's fully charged.

SPECIAL ABILITY:
Electric Play

FAVOURITE GAME: In Flight

EVOLUTION: 14

PROFILES

DORO 27

Restless and playful. He gets nervous when nobody plays.

SPECIAL ABILITY: Valiant Ideas

FAVOURITE GAME: Basket

EVOLUTION: 10

28 DANOKI

Loves to lurk around corners and hide from others.

SPECIAL ABILITY: Camouflage

FAVOURITE GAME: In Flight

EVOLUTION: 12

PROFILES

29 MG-MASK ♂

His head is always in the clouds.
He's a dreamer.

SPECIAL ABILITY:
Imagination

FAVOURITE GAME: On Line

EVOLUTION: 09

♂ GAISOR 30 ♂

Firm and fair. He likes to be
in command of every situation.

SPECIAL ABILITY:
Laser Order

FAVOURITE GAME: Battle

EVOLUTION: 10

PROFILES

LESSEI 31 ♂

Moves his head to the rhythm of any music.

SPECIAL ABILITY:
Rotating Neck

FAVOURITE GAME: K.O.

EVOLUTION: 15

32 POPO ♂

Doesn't like too many bumps but with his lucky star he is a very skilful player.

SPECIAL ABILITY:
Lucky Star

FAVOURITE GAME: Bowling

EVOLUTION: 12

29

NASOKI'S JOKES!

What is worse than a hungry vampire?

A thirsty one!

What did the boy octopus say to the girl octopus on Valentine's Day?

Do you want to hold my hand, hand, hand, hand, hand, hand, hand, hand?

Why didn't the skeleton go to the party?

He had no body to go with!

STARGAZING!

Sully loves to gaze at the stars and discover new things.
Help Sully by joining up the dots in order and then colouring the picture in.

Who knows? You may even discover a new constellation
that you can tell all the other Gogo's about!

GOGO GAMES! GOGO'S® MIX-UP

Those clumsy Gogo's have been packing up their things for a trip and a mix-up has left a few of them without their favourite items. Can you help each of the Gogo's find the way back to their things?

GOGO® JUMBLE

Can you find the Evolution Gogo's hidden in this jumble of letters?

Use the list below to help you find all the Evolution Gogo's names.

```
              F Y C
      U Z E   E L
      R P E   K Q
      R P R   S Q X
      N Q A   S U D
N L C V A K O N E C K Z L M T T U C O R
J O I F E E F O G E E D K R N T X Q O W
Y N E K S S L C T R H A X L J G K T
G P Y U A Z P O G D I N V I I P
Y E P L C I R M D G R O W W
    P Y R S O M M Q L S C K
M O F X S S T O D J P L H I
  X C I M O D H R O Y A J P A
S W P T L Q E W I K O H I O N
N U C H A N S     D K I N X T R
H C K B O K I     J U S O V T T
R W V X L         G J Z J Y
U R G F           V I F A
C O                     L D
```

- ☑ YONOZI
- ☑ FUSO
- ☑ CUPIX
- ☑ HIRCHAN
- ☑ NUCHAN
- ☑ AKONE
- ☑ DANOKI
- ☑ IMOOKI
- ☐ RACETOR
- ☐ TRIKU
- ☑ BOKI
- ☑ FIZER
- ☑ JITTY
- ☑ SKER
- ☐ TUCOR

FIND ALL THE ANSWERS ON PAGE 90

GAME RULES

K.O.

1 Using a piece of chalk, mark a square (or circle) on the floor.

2 Each player must place the same number of Gogo's inside the square. Decide on the number of throws each player will get.

3 Players take turns to stand two metres away and throw a Gogo into the square in an attempt to knock their opponent's Gogo's out of the square.

K.O.

4 If a Gogo gets knocked over but not completely out of the square, it can be put back into position, even if it falls on the line.

5 The winner is the player with the most Gogo's left in the square at the end of the agreed number of throws.

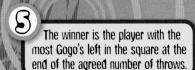

Basket

1. Take a small cardboard or plastic box.

2. Decide how far from the players the box should be.

3. Each player picks five Gogo's of the same colour.

4. Take it in turns to throw a Gogo into the box, making sure it bounces before it goes in.

5. The player who gets the most Gogo's into the box is the winner.

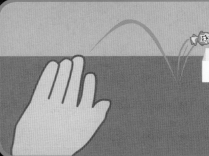

GOGO GAMES!

PUZZLE TROUBLE

Can you complete this jigsaw? Take a look at the pieces littered around the board and see if you can tell which ones finish the jigsaw. Not all of them will fit, so make sure you pick the right ones.

FIND ALL THE ANSWERS ON PAGE 91

HELED'S QUIZ!

1 Who can throw a Gogo higher than anyone else?

A. Migu

B. Sunok

C. Sip

2 What is missing from this Gogo?

A. Their logo

B. An eye

C. Hair

3 Can you name this mixed-up Gogo?

4 If Popo's number is taken away from Mizu's, what is left?

A. 39

B. 23

C. 2

5 Which of these two Gogo's has the smallest evolution according to their evolution bar?

A. Oky

B. Simsei

FIND ALL THE ANSWERS ON PAGE 91

PROFILES

IMOOKI 33

A voice in his earphones tells him the rules of every game. He's got such a terrible memory.

SPECIAL ABILITY:
Voice Recorder

FAVOURITE GAME: Basket

EVOLUTION: 11

34 JEZO

A long losing streak has made this once confident Gogo suddenly very modest.

SPECIAL ABILITY:
Macromodesty

FAVOURITE GAME: Battle

EVOLUTION: 06

PROFILES

EVOLUTION
gogo's
CRAZY BONES

35 SUMI

Full of encouragement. Sumi welcomes everyone with open arms.

SPECIAL ABILITY:
Hugs

FAVOURITE GAME: Scoring

EVOLUTION: 13

SHOON 36

Evolution has made him safety conscious. He likes to slow everyone down.

SPECIAL ABILITY:
Speed Bumps

FAVOURITE GAME: On Line

EVOLUTION: 10

PROFILES

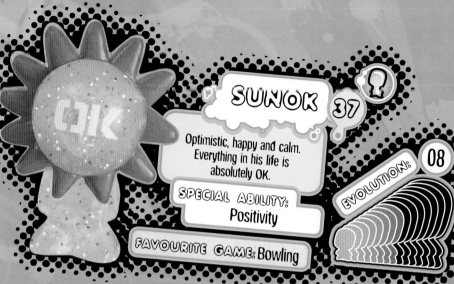

SUNOK 37

Optimistic, happy and calm. Everything in his life is absolutely OK.

SPECIAL ABILITY: Positivity

FAVOURITE GAME: Bowling

EVOLUTION: 08

FIZER 38

Always ready to get the games started.

SPECIAL ABILITY: Ultimate Countdown

FAVOURITE GAME: Basket

EVOLUTION: 07

PROFILES

GAR-GAR 39

Founder of the Gogo's Aerospace Association. Always searching for new horizons.

SPECIAL ABILITY:
Galactic Tourist

FAVOURITE GAME: Basket

EVOLUTION: 12

HAYORI 40

Evolution hasn't changed her vanity. Her hair must always be perfect.

SPECIAL ABILITY:
Hair Styling

FAVOURITE GAME: Basket

EVOLUTION: 04

PROFILES

41 MIGU

The tough guy in the troop. He can throw a Gogo higher than anyone else.

SPECIAL ABILITY: Object Thrower

FAVOURITE GAME: K.O.

EVOLUTION: 08

42 JITTY

Keeps himself cool by flapping his ears.

SPECIAL ABILITY: Cooling Ears

FAVOURITE GAME: In Flight

EVOLUTION: 11

PROFILES

VELOP 43

He can measure his speed and that of any approaching Gogo.

SPECIAL ABILITY:
Speed Gun

FAVOURITE GAME: On Line

EVOLUTION: 09

44 TRIKE

Very happy with his evolution. He has great pride in himself.

SPECIAL ABILITY:
Crushing Hands

FAVOURITE GAME: Battle

EVOLUTION: 10

45 BOKI ♂

A big tummy and a big appetite.
This is one Gogo who is
always on time for a meal.

SPECIAL ABILITY:
Potbelllied Punctuality

FAVOURITE GAME: Basket

EVOLUTION: **10**

CHIMU ♂ 46

Never afraid to get hurt.
This is one Gogo who is ready
for any daring challenge.

SPECIAL ABILITY:
Rubber Stop

FAVOURITE GAME: On Line

EVOLUTION: **06**

PROFILES

DUOP 47

A real split personality. You'd better be careful with how much you trust him.

SPECIAL ABILITY: Two-Face

FAVOURITE GAME: Bowling

EVOLUTION: 05

TUBOR 48

Always alert and always aware. His senses are even higher when he sleeps.

SPECIAL ABILITY: Hyper Attention

FAVOURITE GAME: On Line

EVOLUTION: 07

HELED'S QUIZ!

1 I have an evolution number of 11, I love to play Basket and I wear headphones. Who am I?

2  What is wrong with this picture of Pilhy?

A. Too many eyes ☐

B. Teeth too big ☐

C. Stripe wrong colour ☐

3 How many eyelashes does E-Flo have?

4 Can you name the two Gogo's who have got into a bit of a mix-up here?

A.

B.

5 You are placing Gogo's a hand-width from a wall – what game are you playing?

A. Baseball ☐

B. Crazy Touch ☐

C. Bowling ☐

FIND ALL THE ANSWERS ON PAGE 92

GOGO® WORD

GOGO® GAMES!

No idea about Naskoki? Clueless about Kam? Time to test your Evolution Gogo's Crazy Bones knowledge with a little brain teaser.

Don't worry if you are not a complete Evolution expert – all the answers can be found in this book.

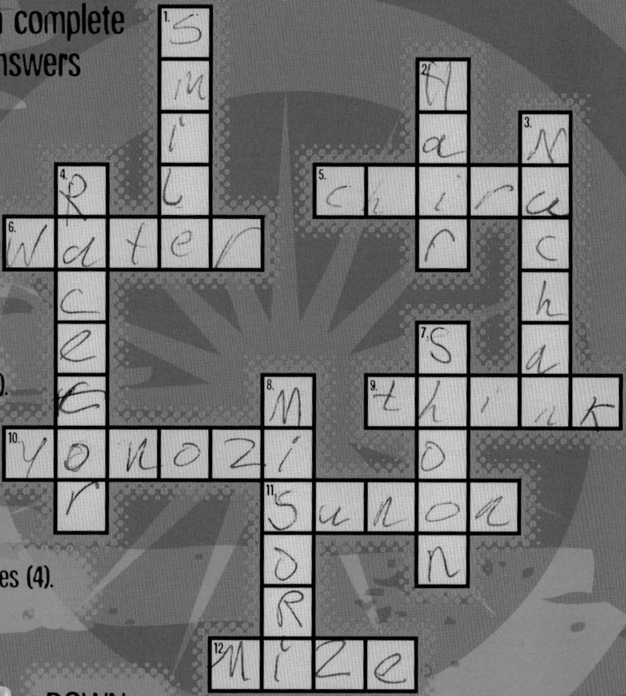

ACROSS

5. Which Gogo loves counting sheep? (5).
6. Snok spends long hours under the what? (5).
9. Heled can do what super-fast? (5).
10. Solve the anagram NOZYOI to find this Gogo's name (6).
11. Which Gogo is extremely ticklish? (5).
12. He locks on his target with his eyes (4).

DOWN

1. Skimy is known for his happy what? (5).
2. Hayori is always known for having perfect what? (4).
3. Who acts like the chief Gogo? (6).
4. His love of sports cars is reflected in his name. (7).
7. He doesn't like speed and tries to slow everyone down. (5).
8. Which Gogo is lacking in confidence? (6).

FIND ALL THE ANSWERS ON PAGE 92

GOGO GAMES!

FAWA'S PHOTO

As the official photographer of the Gogo's, Fawa loves discovering new things to take pictures of. While on a recent photography trip he found a whole new group of Gogo's.

Sadly his camera got damaged and he didn't get all the pictures. Use your drawing and colouring skills to design some new Gogo's and help Fawa show everyone his amazing pictures.

FOUL-UP!

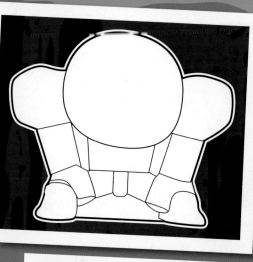

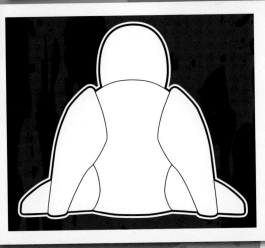

GOGO GAMES! COLOUR MY GOGO

Today seems to be a bit of a dull day for the Evolution Gogo's Crazy Bones. Use your pencils and pens to add some colour back to the picture below.

SATORI'S SPOT-IT

Satori is known for his talents of observation. The Gogo's are sure there is something wrong with their pictures and are relying on you and Satori to sort it out.

Can you spot the 10 differences between the two pictures. Satori's reputation as the most watchful Gogo is on the line so make sure you find them all.

FIND ALL THE ANSWERS ON PAGE 93

GAME RULES

In flight

① Players decide before starting how many rounds will be played. Place four Gogo's on the floor in a square shape and place a fifth one in the middle.

② Take the Gogo from the middle and throw it into the air. Now try to pick up as many of the other Gogo's as you can before catching the Gogo you threw.

③ You must throw and catch the Gogo with the same hand you use to pick up the other Gogo's.

④ If the player doesn't catch the Gogo they threw up into the air, then no points are scored. Players get a point for every Gogo they pick up and the winner is the player with the most points at the end of all the rounds.

GAME RULES

on line

1 Use any line on the ground or draw one yourself. Each player throws a Gogo without dragging it.

2 The player who manages to throw their Gogo nearest the line wins the throw.

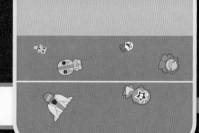

3 If a player manages to get a Gogo directly on the line they score double points.

4 The player who wins the most throws wins the game.

PROFILES

49 CUPIX

Uses his screen face to play Gogo games with his friends.

SPECIAL ABILITY:
Game Player

FAVOURITE GAME: K.O.

EVOLUTION: 08

B-KORI 50

He's so friendly that his horns don't scare anybody.

SPECIAL ABILITY:
Makes Friends

FAVOURITE GAME: Battle

EVOLUTION: 07

51 CROOKI

An electric shock has left him fully charged.

SPECIAL ABILITY: Electro-Smile

FAVOURITE GAME: Scoring

EVOLUTION: 06

FUSO 52

A wild dancer. He makes moves that others couldn't even imagine.

SPECIAL ABILITY: Music Fever

FAVOURITE GAME: Scoring

EVOLUTION: 06

PROFILES

EGOR 53

The hungriest Gogo of all. Keeps his mouth wide open for instant snacking.

SPECIAL ABILITY: Ultimate Eating

FAVOURITE GAME: Basket

EVOLUTION: 07

TARI 54

Never play hide-and-seek with Tari. He wins every time.

SPECIAL ABILITY: Bionic Eye

FAVOURITE GAME: K.O.

EVOLUTION: 09

PROFILES

55 E-FLO

This Gogo loves nature, wildlife and outdoor adventures.

SPECIAL ABILITY:
Exploration

FAVOURITE GAME: K.O.

EVOLUTION: 10

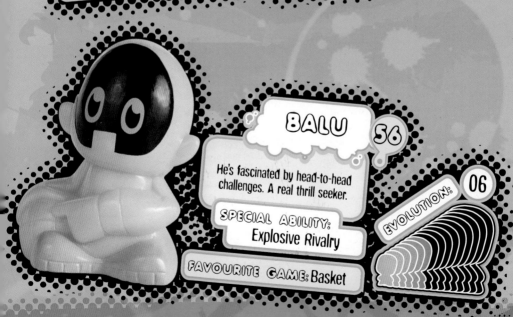

BALU 56

He's fascinated by head-to-head challenges. A real thrill seeker.

SPECIAL ABILITY:
Explosive Rivalry

FAVOURITE GAME: Basket

EVOLUTION: 06

57 YONOZI ♂

Likes to get everything arranged in perfect order. Every detail is double checked.

SPECIAL ABILITY:
Organization

FAVOURITE GAME: Battle

EVOLUTION: 08

58 EKEN ♂

He's got an anti-bump position which makes him extra hard to tumble down.

SPECIAL ABILITY:
Solid Stance

FAVOURITE GAME: Basket

EVOLUTION: 07

PROFILES

KALIN 59

EVOLUTION: 06

An important Gogo who carries news and information to the others.

SPECIAL ABILITY:
Gogo's Representative

FAVOURITE GAME: In Flight

60 KINGO

EVOLUTION: 13

A body that looks like a face, a face that looks like a body. . .some Gogo's don't know what to make of him.

SPECIAL ABILITY:
Body-Face

FAVOURITE GAME: Battle

FAWA ♂ **61**

The official photographer. Always ready to capture a key moment.

SPECIAL ABILITY:
Photographic Vision

FAVOURITE GAME: K.O.

EVOLUTION: **06**

62 ## FANTU ♂

When it's time for him to play, he's so happy that his eye starts dancing.

SPECIAL ABILITY:
Restless Eye

FAVOURITE GAME: Basket

EVOLUTION: **03**

PROFILES

63 **TUCOR** ♂

A sore loser but really he
has a kind heart.

SPECIAL ABILITY:
Grumpy Smiles

FAVOURITE GAME: K.O.

EVOLUTION: **08**

♂ **SUT** **64** ♀

Sometimes he walks like a zombie.
Sleeping problems maybe?

SPECIAL ABILITY:
Zombie Trance

FAVOURITE GAME: In Flight

EVOLUTION: **09**

BOWLING

1 Each player must place the same number of Gogo's on the floor, about a hands-width (with fingers spread) from the wall.

2 Take it in turns to throw a Gogo and knock over as many of your opponent's Gogo's as you can.

3 It doesn't matter if you knock down one of your own Gogo's: stand it up and carry on with the game. The player who knocks down the greatest number of their opponent's Gogo's wins the game.

GAME RULES

1 Before you start, players must decide how many rounds they want to play.

Bone Flip

2 The first player places three Gogo's in the palm of their hand, then throws them up into the air a short distance.

3 While the Gogo's are in the air, the player flips their hand over and tries to catch as many Gogo's as they can on the back of their hand. A point is scored for each Gogo successfully caught.

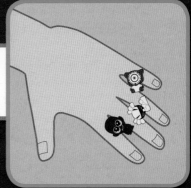

4 The next player takes their turn and this completes one round. Add another Gogo for each round that is played.

5 The winner is the player with the most points at the end of all the rounds.

GOGO GAMES!

GOGO® CRAZY

By now you should know the Gogo's inside out, left to right and upside down, so drawing them should be easy for you.

Use the grid for reference and once you are done, don't forget to add plenty of colour to your creation.

TUBOR >

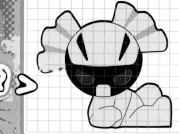

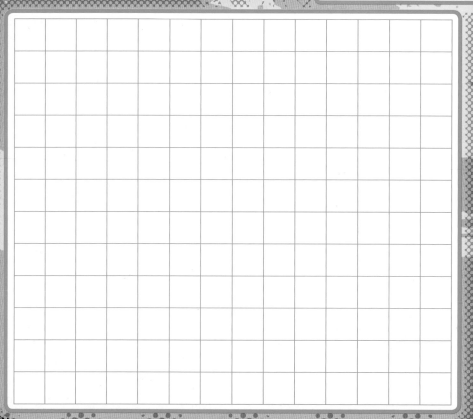

DOODLE-DO!

< AKONE >

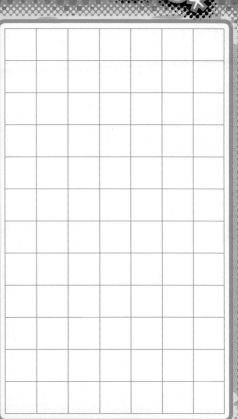

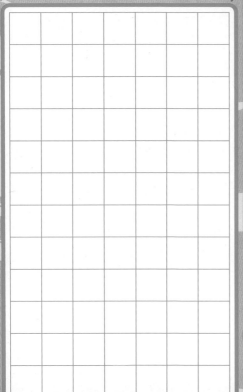

HIRCHAN >

HELED'S QUIZ!

1 Which Gogo concentrates the water supply to put out fires?

- A. Zuy ☐
- B. Nebub ☐
- C. Jezo ☐

2

What is wrong with this picture of Mizu?

- A. Wrong head ☐
- B. Missing eye ☐
- C. Wrong colour ☐

3

Which Gogo couldn't bear to be seen without this logo?

☐

4 I have glowing glasses, I love to play battle and I have a particle searcher ability. Who am I?

- A. Mc-Mask ☐
- B. Narion ☐
- C. Tubor ☐

5 Can you untangle the name of the Gogo below?

Ⓤ Ⓡ Ⓒ Ⓔ Ⓢ Ⓡ

☐ ☐ ☐ ☐ ☐ ☐

FIND ALL THE ANSWERS ON PAGE 93

NASOKI'S JOKES!

What is a cat's favourite colour?

Purrple!

What is a volcano?

A mountain with hiccups!

What kind of hair do oceans have?

Wavy!

GAME RULES

1
Players choose the number of Gogo's to be used. This can be anything from one to five Gogo's at a time.

SCORING

2
Each player takes turns to throw their Gogo's on the floor.

I'M SO EVO

3
Using the chart below, work out your score by looking at how the Gogo's land.

4
Each player has three goes and the one with the highest score at the end wins. Of course, you can take more turns if you are looking for a longer game!

SCORE CHART

5 POINTS	2 POINTS	1 POINTS	0 POINTS

Hand Bone

1 Each player takes a number of Gogo's in their hand without letting the other player see how many.

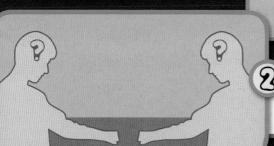

2 With their hands closed, each player tries to guess how many Gogo's the other player has in their hand.

3 If you guess correctly that your opponent has three Gogo's in their hand, then you win three points. If you guess incorrectly, then you lose three points (or points equal to the number of Gogo's in their hand).

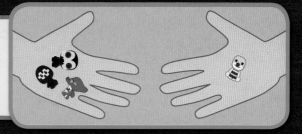

4 The winner is the first player to reach a score of 20.

TIP Expert players can try to guess not only the number but also which Gogo's the other player has in their hand.

PROFILES

TAKI 65

Covers his eyes to train his sense of smell. He's always right.

SPECIAL ABILITY:
Canine Sense of Smell

FAVOURITE GAME: On Line

EVOLUTION: 10

66 SKIMY

He just wants to play games all day long. Never too tired to play.

SPECIAL ABILITY:
Happy Smile

FAVOURITE GAME: K.O.

EVOLUTION: 14

PROFILES

67 **KAM**

Obsessed with his music.
Talk loudly if you want
his attention.

SPECIAL ABILITY:
Musical Ear

FAVOURITE GAME: On Line

EVOLUTION: 07

FLICK 68

It's impossible to knock
him down if you look
straight into his eyes.

SPECIAL ABILITY:
Hypnosis

FAVOURITE GAME: In Flight

EVOLUTION: 09

69 SIP ♂

Looks like he has bad eyesight but his aim is perfect every time.

SPECIAL ABILITY:
Hitting the Target

FAVOURITE GAME: Bowling

EVOLUTION: 06

TRIKU 70 ♂

Pays good attention to the game...
from the front, left and right.

SPECIAL ABILITY:
Triple Vision

FAVOURITE GAME: Bowling

EVOLUTION: 07

EVOLUTION **gogo's** CRAZY BONES

MIZU 71

Locks the target with his eyes and fires straight down the middle.

SPECIAL ABILITY:
Mizu Straight Throw

FAVOURITE GAME: On Line

EVOLUTION: 07

72 VATCO

Wants to eat something. . . but doesn't know what.

SPECIAL ABILITY:
Unknown Appetite

FAVOURITE GAME: Battle

EVOLUTION: 10

73 **MAKA**

A true individual. Happy with his unusual looks.

SPECIAL ABILITY:
Paints Clouds

FAVOURITE GAME: Scoring

EVOLUTION: **14**

FEMO **74**

He can't wait to join GAR-GAR's Aerospace Association.

SPECIAL ABILITY:
UFO Detector

FAVOURITE GAME: Scoring

EVOLUTION: **13**

PROFILES

75 **CRUSER**

Performs great magic tricks, even though he can't hide anything.

SPECIAL ABILITY:
Transparent Magic Tricks

FAVOURITE GAME: Scoring

EVOLUTION: 08

MISORI **76**

Lacking in confidence but always plays better than expected.

SPECIAL ABILITY:
Ear-Antenna

FAVOURITE GAME: Scoring

EVOLUTION: 09

ZUY 77

He thinks that he'll win every game. . . unfortunately, he suffers a lot of disappointment.

SPECIAL ABILITY:
Winning Spirit

FAVOURITE GAME: K.O.

EVOLUTION: 11

TIN-CHU 78

Always proposing some foul play. Loves wrestling.

SPECIAL ABILITY:
Tin-Chu Chop

FAVOURITE GAME: Battle

EVOLUTION: 06

PROFILES

79

SNOK ♂

Spends long hours under water. Everybody goes crazy looking for him.

SPECIAL ABILITY:
Deep Breathing

FAVOURITE GAME: Bowling

EVOLUTION: **12**

80

KIVU ♂

Carefully concentrates his thoughts before any attack.

SPECIAL ABILITY:
Concentration

FAVOURITE GAME: In Flight

EVOLUTION: **11**

EVO GOGO'S®

It's time to do a little evolving of your own. The evolution machine at the Gogo's factory has broken down and they need your help to continue their work.

Take a look at the each of the Gogo's due to evolve and use your drawing skills to make a new Gogo from the two existing ones.

We've given you an example to get you started but the colours and designs are completely up to you.

FUN FACTORY

EVO GOGO'S®

FUN FACTORY

GOGO GAMES!

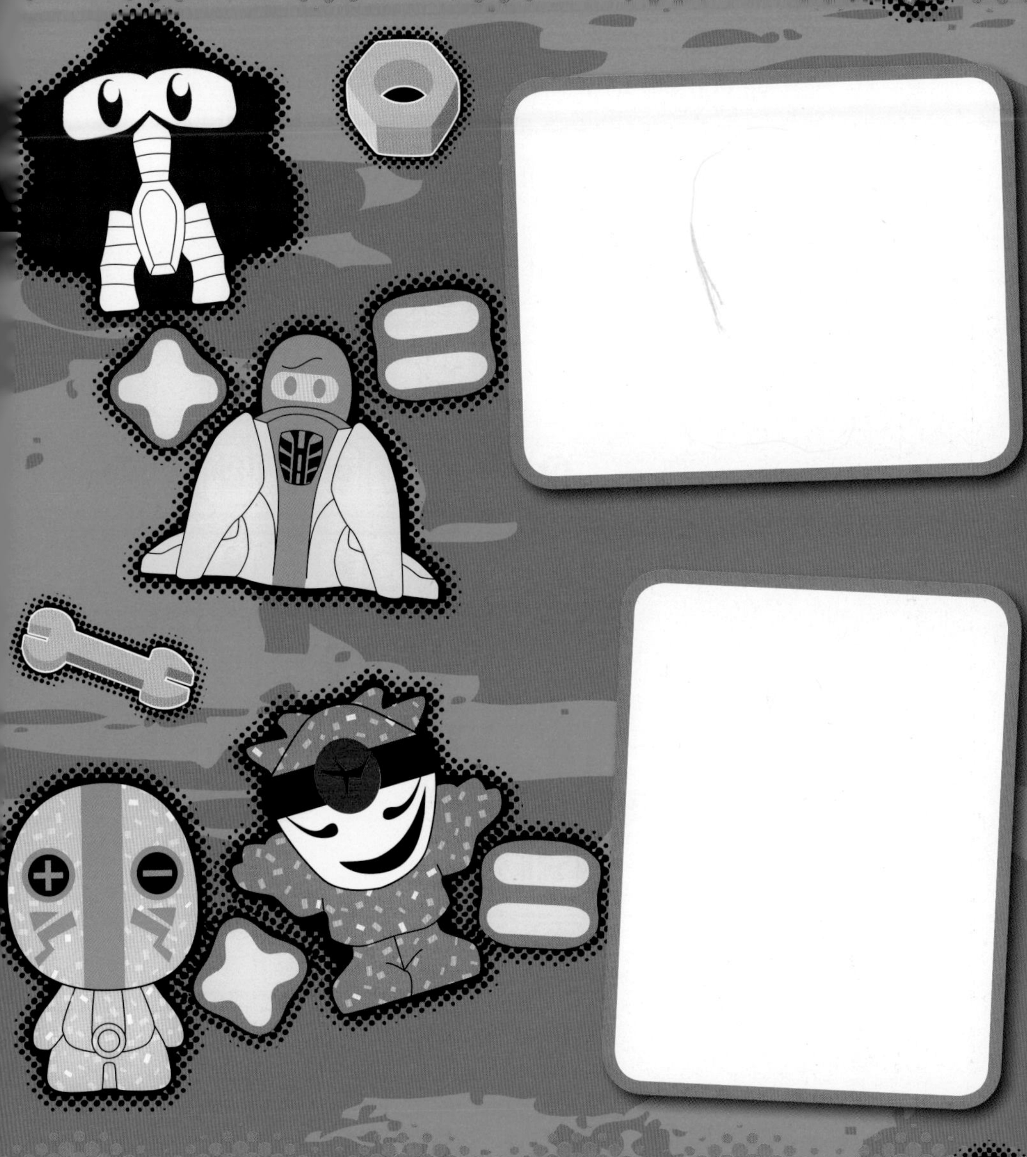

EVOLUTION GOGO'S CRAZY BONES — CHECKLIST

Have you got all the Gogo's? This is a list of all the Evolution Gogo's Crazy Bones® available. Use it to keep track of the ones you've got and the ones you still need to collect.

 01 MOSHI

02 NASOKI

03 SATORI

04 OKY

05 RACETOR

06 HELED

07 SKER

08 ANGOR

09 TAI-UMU

10 KOKU-CHAN

83

EVOLUTION GOGO'S CRAZY BONES CHECKLIST

25 TEMSEI

26 PILHY

27 DORO

28 DANOKI

29 MC-MASK

30 GAISOR

31 LESSEI

32 POPO

33 IMOOKI

34 JEZO

35 SUMI

36 SHOON

37 SUNOK

38 FIZER

84

39	GAR-GAR		X		X		X		X		X
40	HAYORI		X		X		X		X		X
41	MIGU		X		X		X		X		X
42	JITTY		X		X		X		X		X
43	VELOP		X		X		X		X		X
44	TRIKE		X		X		X		X		X
45	BOKI		X		X		X		X		X

46	CHIMU		X		X		X		X		X
47	DUOP		X		X		X		X		X
48	TUBOR		X		X		X		X		X

49	CUPIX		X		X		X		X		X
50	B-KORI		X		X		X		X		X
51	CROOKI		X		X		X		X		X

52	FUSO		X		X		X		X		X

53 EGOR

54 TARI

55 E-FLO

56 BALU

57 YONOZI

58 EKEN

59 KALIN

60 KINGO

61 FAWA

62 FANTU

63 TUCOR

64 SUT

65 TAKI

66 SKIMY

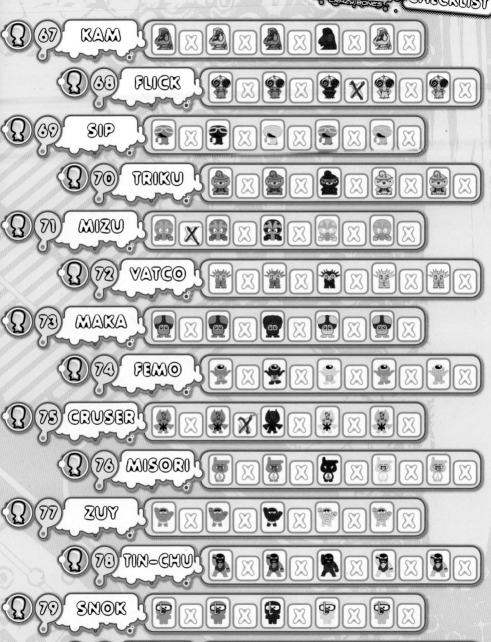

ANSWERS – ANSWERS

 = 12

 = 13

 = 13

 = 10

 = 7

1. A. Yonozi
2. Snok
3. Eken
4. C. Egor
5. Battle

16 GOGO GAMES! THE GOGO' SUSPECTS

1. KOKU-CHAN
2. AKONE
3. CUPIX
4. SIMSEI
5. MOSHI X
6. NASOKI

20 HELED'S QUIZ!

1. Cupix and Sut
2. B. Kivu
3. C. 96
4. Jitty
5. Manic Hair

21 * GOGO GAMES! LOST GOGO'S

33 * GOGO GAMES! GOGO JUMBLE

36 GOGO GAMES! PUZZLE TROUBLE

37 HELED'S QUIZ!

1. A. Migu
2. B. An eye
3. Hayori
4. A. 39
5. B. Simsei

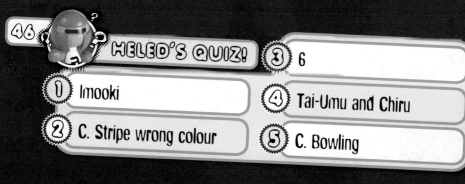

46 HELED'S QUIZ!

1. Imooki
2. C. Stripe wrong colour
3. 6
4. Tai-Umu and Chiru
5. C. Bowling

47 GOGO GAMES! GOGO' WORD

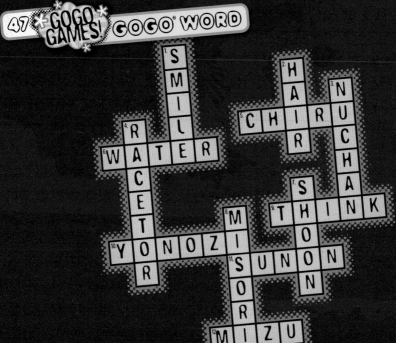

51 *GOGO GAMES!* SATORI'S SPOT IT

66 HELED'S QUIZ!

1 B. Nebub

2 B. Missing eye

3 Sunok

4 B. Narion

5 Cruser

EVOLUTION gogo's CRAZY BONES® Official HANDBOOK²

GOGO'S CRAZY BONES® EVOLUTION OFFICIAL HANDBOOK 2
A BANTAM BOOK 978 0 553 82097 3
First published in Great Britain by Bantam
An imprint of Random House Children's Books
A Random House Group Company
This edition published 2009
1 2 3 4 5 6 7 8 9 10

Bantam Books are published by Random House Children's Books,
61-63 Uxbridge Road, London W5 5SA
www.rbooks.co.uk
www.kidsatrandomhouse.co.uk
Addresses for companies within The Random house Group Limited can be found at:
www.randomhouse.co.uk/offices.htm
THE RANDOM HOUSE GROUP Limited Reg. No. 954009
A CIP catalogue record for this book is available from the British Library
Printed in Italy

MAGIC BOX INT.®

ppi Worldwide